Handcrafted Ornaments

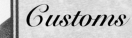

Christmas *Customs*

Handcrafted Ornaments

**CREATIVE
PUBLISHING**
international

MINNETONKA, MINNESOTA

Copyright © 2001
Creative Publishing international, Inc.
5900 Green Oak Drive
Minnetonka, Minnesota 55343
1-800-328-3895
All rights reserved.
www.howtobookstore.com

President/CEO: David D. Murphy

CHRISTMAS CUSTOMS: HANDCRAFTED ORNAMENTS
Created by the editors of Creative Publishing international.

Executive Editor: Elaine Perry
Senior Editor: Linda Neubauer
Senior Art Director: Stephanie Michaud
Art Director: Mark Jacobson
Desktop Publishing Specialist: Laurie Kristensen
Project & Prop Stylist: Joanne Wawra
Samplemaker: Arlene Dohrman
Photographer: Tate Carlson
Director of Production Services: Kim Gerber

Creative Publishing international, Inc. offers a variety of how-to
books. For information write:
   Creative Publishing international, Inc.
     Subscriber Books
   5900 Green Oak Drive
   Minnetonka, MN 55343

ISBN 1-58923-011-6

Printed in Singapore
10 9 8 7 6 5 4 3 2 1

Table of Contents

ong revered for its ability to remain green and alive in the dead of winter, the fir tree has been a symbol of eternity, hope, and promise since the dawn of time. Believing that evil would not go wherever the fir tree was, pagans brought them into their homes. Early Christians kept the custom, transferring the hope and promise of Christmas to the symbolic tree.

The first Christmas trees were small, usually set up on a table, with beeswax candles clipped to their branches. Their decorations included food items and tiny, inexpensive gifts that symbolized an aspect of the Christmas spirit. Today, the custom of bringing a fir tree into the home, stringing it with lights, and hanging ornaments from its branches is so central to the observance of Christmas, that we do it year after year without really understanding why. Perhaps along the way we have lost sight of the origin and symbolic meaning behind this age-old custom. Modern-day Christmas tree ornaments include everything from plain glass balls to velvet-clad elves, and trees are often decked out in kitschy themes—smothered in feathers, swathed with pink netting, or dripping with gold beads. Yet, there are a few handcrafted ornaments that have lasting significance and a story to tell.

Apples

Religious theater began in the Middle Ages, perhaps in the 11th century. One of the most popular plays in Germany at that time was the story of Adam and Eve in the Garden of Eden. In the center of the stage stood an apple tree, a symbol of the Tree of Good and Evil, or the Tree of Life. Because the play ended with the prophesy of a coming Savior, it became very popular during the Advent season. Unable to find an apple tree full of fruit in the dead of winter, the stagehands would decorate a fir tree with apples. Eventually, this piece of scenery became known as the Paradise Tree and was a well-recognized symbol of Christmas. The custom endured, and the Christmas tree was born; its first ornaments were apples.

The Christmas Rose

Wonder and awe at the birth of the Christ Child filled her heart as Madelon, a young shepherdess, hurried to shelter her sheep from the wintry night wind. Wise Men from the East passed her by, carrying rich gifts of spices and gold to honor the baby. Fellow shepherds made gifts of fruits and honey. Her excitement turned to sadness as the poor girl realized that she had nothing to give. She stood outside the stable and wept. As her tears fell on the snow at her feet, a vigilant angel swept away the snow to reveal a beautiful white rose tipped with pink. Madelon wiped away her tears, picked the rose, and presented it as her gift to the Newborn King.

The Christmas rose still blooms in the snowy mountains of central Europe during the holiday season. It has become a custom to plant the rose by the front door to welcome Christ. Fittingly, roses fashioned from delicate ribbons can add an elegant touch to the Christmas tree or adorn holiday gifts.

How to make a Traditional Christmas Rose

Ribbon roses are constructed using either standard ribbon for a traditional rose or wired ribbon for a cabbage-style rose, and are secured to wire stems. The stems are wrapped with floral tape, with artificial leaves inserted for a finishing touch. Make roses of different sizes, using ribbon in different widths.

The length of the ribbon needed for each rose varies with the width of the ribbon and the desired finished size. A rose made with ⅝" (1.5 cm) ribbon may require ½ yd. (0.5 m) of ribbon, while a rose made with 2¼" (6 cm) ribbon may require 1½ yd. (1.4 m) of ribbon.

Materials

- Medium-gauge stem wire.
- Fine-gauge paddle floral wire.
- Ribbon in desired width; width of ribbon and desired finished size of rose determine the length needed.
- Artificial rose leaves.
- Floral tape.

1

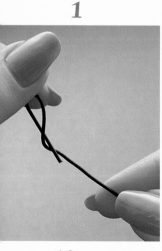

2

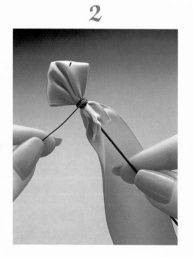

3

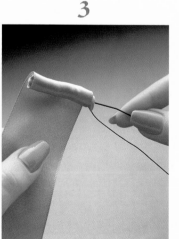

4

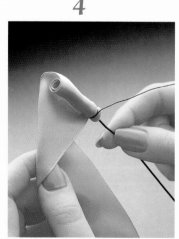

1 Bend a 1" (2.5 cm) loop in the end of stem wire; twist to secure.

2 Fold ribbon end over loop; wrap with paddle floral wire to secure.

3 Hold ribbon taut in left hand and stem wire in right hand; roll stem wire toward left hand, wrapping ribbon tightly around the fold three times, forming rose center. Wrap paddle wire tightly around base to secure.

4 Fold ribbon back diagonally as shown, close to rose. Roll rose center over fold, keeping upper edge of rose center just below upper edge of fold; lower edges of ribbon will not be aligned.

5 Roll to end of fold, forming petal. Wrap paddle wire tightly around base.

6 Repeat steps 4 and 5 for desired number of petals. Fold ribbon back diagonally, and secure with paddle wire at base; cut ribbon and paddle wire.

7 Wrap end of floral tape around base of rose, stretching tape slightly for best adhesion. Wrap entire base of rose, concealing wire. Continue wrapping floral tape onto stem wire. Place stem of artificial rose leaf next to stem wire; wrap stem wire and leaf stem together with floral tape. Continue wrapping until entire stem wire is covered with floral tape.

5

6

7

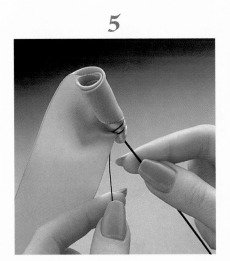

How to make a Cabbage-Style Rose

Materials

- Medium-gauge stem wire.
- Wired ribbon in desired width; width of ribbon and desired finished size of rose determine length needed.
- Artificial rose leaves.
- Floral tape.

1

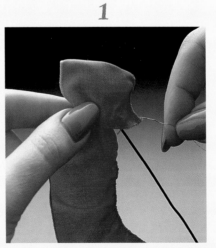

2

14

1 Follow step 1 on page 13. Cut a 1 to 1½ yd. (0.95 to 1.4 m) length of wired ribbon. Pull out about 2" (5 cm) of wire on one edge of one end of ribbon. Fold ribbon end over loop; secure with pulled wire, forming rose center.

2 Gather up one edge of remaining length of ribbon tightly by sliding ribbon along ribbon wire toward the rose center.

3 Wrap the gathered edge around the base of the rose, wrapping each layer slightly higher than the previous layer.

4 Fold the ribbon end down and catch under last layer. Wrap ribbon wire tightly around base several times to secure. Cut off excess ribbon wire.

5 Follow step 7 on page 13, covering gathered edge of ribbon and wire.

3

4

5

15

Hand-Cast Paper

Chinese people were making and using paper for nearly a thousand years before anyone else. At first, they chopped up old fishing nets, suspended the fibers in water, felted them onto a screen, and dried them in the hot sun. Knowledge of the process began to spread slowly through Africa and Europe in the 8th century but didn't reach England until 1494, two years after Columbus sailed to America. The first U.S. paper mill, built in 1690, produced handmade paper from old, shredded and soaked linen and cotton rags. Once mechanized, worldwide paper production and use skyrocketed. Just stop to think of all the uses for paper!

Eventually, hand-making paper once again became a treasured art form. During the Victorian era, when heavily decorated Christmas trees were in fashion, people sought a way to make lightweight decorations that would not strain the tree branches. Inexpensive and lightweight, paper solved the problem. Artisans made figures and medallions by pressing wet paper pulp into molds intended for cookies or chocolates.

How to make a Hand-Cast Paper Ornament

Though they may appear to be very delicate, these hand-cast paper ornaments are durable enough to become lasting keepsakes. Dried ornaments may be painted, using watercolor paints, or shaded, using chalk pastels. Tiny sprigs of dried floral material and narrow ribbons may be added. For sparkle, fine glitter may be applied.

Supplies for making hand-cast paper ornaments are available at craft or art supply stores. One sheet of cotton linter measuring 8" × 7" (20.5 × 18 cm) will produce enough pulp for three ornaments. Preparation of the ceramic mold before casting may vary with each brand; read manufacturer's instructions before beginning the project.

Leftover pulp can be saved for later use. Squeeze out excess water, and spread the pulp out in small clumps to dry. It is not necessary to add more paper-casting powder when resoaking and processing leftover pulp.

Materials

- Cotton linter.
- Household blender.
- Paper-casting powder, such as paper clay or paper additive.
- Strainer.
- Ceramic casting mold.
- Sponge; kitchen towel.
- Watercolor paints or chalk pastels, optional.

- Cord or narrow ribbon, for hanger; darning needle, for inserting hanger.
- Embellishments, such as dried floral materials, narrow ribbons, and glitter, optional.
- Craft glue, or hot glue gun and glue sticks, optional.

1

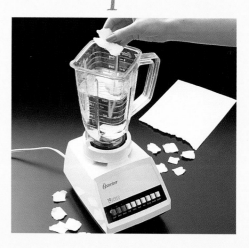

1 Tear 8" × 7" (20.5 × 18 cm) sheet of cotton linter into 1" (2.5 cm) pieces. Put in the blender with 1 quart (1 L) water; allow to soak for several minutes.

2 Blend the water and linter for 30 seconds on low speed. Add 1 teaspoon (5 mL) of paper-casting powder to mixture; blend on high speed for one minute.

3 Pour about one-third of mixture into strainer, draining off water. Put wet pulp into mold.

4 Spread pulp evenly around mold and out onto flat outer edges; pulp on flat edges will form deckled edge around border of ornament.

5 Press damp sponge over pulp, compressing it into the mold and drawing off excess water; wring out sponge. Repeat two or three times until excess water is removed.

6 Press a folded kitchen towel over the compressed pulp, absorbing any remaining water and further compressing pulp.

7 Allow compressed pulp to dry completely in the mold. To speed drying, place the mold in an oven heated to 150°F (65°C) for about three hours.

8 Loosen deckled edge of border around hand-cast paper ornament, using blade of knife; gently remove ornament from mold.

9 Thread cord or narrow ribbon into darning needle. Insert the needle through top of ornament at inner edge of border; knot ends of cord. Embellish ornament as desired:

Paint hand-cast paper ornaments, using diluted watercolors and small brush. Allow a painted area to dry before painting the adjacent area.

Color-shade hand-cast paper ornaments, using chalk pastels or cosmetic powders. Apply with small brush or small foam applicator.

Glitter by outlining or filling in small areas, using glitter glue in fine-tip tubes. Or, for large areas, apply glue over areas, using glue pen or glue stick. Sprinkle with glitter; shake off excess.

3

5

9

Scherenschnitte

Long before German and Austrian craftsmen claimed this art form as their own, intricate paper cuttings were made in China. There paper cuttings were used for ceremonial purposes, to honor political leaders and to record the history of the Chinese people. Later German and Austrian artists adopted the craft to make lightweight decorations for the Christmas tree. They called it *scherenschnitte* (shear-en-shnit-tah), or scissors' cuttings. Delicate filigrees of carefully cut paper depict various scenes and symbols of the Christmas story.

How to make
Scherenschnitte Ornaments

These paper cuttings can be displayed as a single, flat ornament or a garland of repeated motifs. Two identical scherenschnitte pieces can be made and sewn together down the center for a three-dimensional ornament. Several patterns for each style are given on pages 62 and 63. Ornaments can be antiqued, if desired, or painted with watercolor paints. For added sparkle, glitter may be applied to the ornament.

Choose art papers that have a sharp edge when cut. Parchment papers are particularly suitable for scherenschnitte, due to their strength and ability to accept stain or watercolors. Scissors with short, sharp, pointed blades are necessary for the intricate work of scherenschnitte. Tiny detail cutting on the interior of the design is easier to do with a mat knife and cutting surface.

Materials

- Art paper.
- Tracing paper.
- Graphite paper, for transferring design.
- Scissors with short, sharp, pointed blades.
- Mat knife and cutting surface.
- Needle; thread, for hanger.
- Removable tape; scrap of corrugated cardboard; pushpin.
- Instant coffee and cotton-tipped swab, for antiquing, optional.
- Watercolor paints and glitter, optional.

1

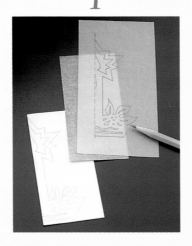

2

1 **Single ornament.** Cut a piece of art paper larger than the pattern dimensions (pages 62 and 63); for a symmetrical design, fold paper in half, right sides together. Trace pattern onto tracing paper. Transfer the design from tracing paper to wrong side of folded art paper, using graphite paper; align the dotted line on design to fold of art paper.

2 Tape folded art paper to cutting surface, placing the tape in area outside design. Cut out interior shapes using mat knife; begin with shapes nearest fold, and work toward edges of paper. Make any small holes by punching through paper with a needle.

3 Remove art paper from cutting surface, and cut outer edge of design with scissors. Open cut design.

4 Press flat with a warm iron. Antique or embellish as desired, using one of the three methods on page 25. Attach thread hanger at center of the ornament 1/4" (6 mm) from the upper edge, using a hand needle; knot the thread ends.

1 **Three-dimensional ornament.** Follow steps 1 to 4 for two identical designs, omitting thread hanger. Place the cut designs on top of each other, aligning edges; secure to scrap of corrugated cardboard, using removable tape. Punch holes with pushpin every 1/4" (6 mm) along the center fold, through both layers.

2 Thread a needle with 18" (46 cm) length of thread in same color as ornament. Sew in and out of holes from top to bottom of ornament. Turn ornament over, and stitch back up to top hole. Tie the ends of thread together at desired length for hanger. Arrange the ornament sections at right angles to each other.

3

4

1

2

*H*ow to make a
Scherenschnitte Garland

1 Cut strip of art paper 11" (28 cm) long and 2¾" (7 cm) wide. Fold in half, wrong sides together, to make 5½" × 4¼" (14 × 10.8 cm) strip. Fold short ends to center fold, right sides together, so the strip is accordion-folded, with wrong side facing out.

2 Trace design for garland (page 63) onto tracing paper. Transfer design from tracing paper to wrong side of folded art paper, using graphite paper; align dotted lines on design to double-folded edges of paper.

3 Cut out the design, following steps 2 and 3 for single ornament on page 23. Open out garland. Embellish, if desired, using one of the three methods opposite.

4 Repeat steps 1 to 3 as necessary to make as many garland lengths as desired. Press the garland pieces flat with a warm iron. Join garland lengths with small pieces of tape on wrong side.

1

2

How to embellish Scherenschnitte Ornaments

Watercolor painted ornaments. Paint scherenschnitte ornament with watercolor paint and soft brush. Allow to dry; press with warm iron. Repeat on back side.

Glittered ornaments. Apply glue over areas to be glittered, using glue pen. Sprinkle with glitter; shake off the excess. Repeat on back side.

Antiqued ornaments. Mix 1½ teaspoons (7 mL) instant coffee with ½ cup (125 mL) hot water. Apply coffee to outer edge of ornament and around large openings with cotton swab. Allow to dry; press. Repeat on back side.

Baskets

askets of any shape or form are a common Christmas tree decoration. As part of the hospitality of the season, they often hold sweet treats and are taken from the tree and given to holiday guests. The basket and its tiny presents represent the crèche and God's gift of the Christ Child. Scandinavian cone-shaped baskets are one example. Simple in design, these baskets most likely originated as a paper craft to help children learn about the Christmas story. More elaborate styles evolved, including fabric cones with gimp trims, beads, and tassels.

How to sew a Basket Ornament

Decorate your tree with elegant basket ornaments trimmed with a combination of ribbons, braid trims, and tassels, beads, or buttons. Select from two versions of the basket ornament, both made from dress-weight fabrics such as silks, satins, and brocades. One style is made from a single outer fabric. The other version is made from several pieced fabrics for a patchwork effect. The baskets can be stuffed with miniature Christmas ornaments and packages. Or they can be filled with wrapped candies. The baskets measure 6" (15 cm) high, not including the tassel or hanger.

Cutting Directions: Cut one 7" (18 cm) square from outer fabric or from pieced outer fabric (opposite, steps 1 and 2) and lining fabric and two 7" (18 cm) squares from fusible interfacing. Cut one piece of heavyweight nonfusible interfacing, using pattern (page 62).

Materials

- ¼ yd. (0.25 m) outer basket fabric; or scraps of four or five fabrics, for pieced outer basket.
- ¼ yd. (0.25 m) lining fabric.
- ¼ yd. (0.25 m) fusible knit interfacing.

- Scrap of heavyweight nonfusible interfacing.
- ¼ yd. (0.25 m) each of trims, for the outer rim and inner rim of basket.
- ¼ yd. (0.25 m) trim, to cover seam, optional.

- ¼ yd. (0.25 m) ribbon or braid trim, for basket hanger.
- Liquid fray preventer.
- Tassel, beads, or button, optional.
- Miniature ornaments, packages, or wrapped candies, to fill basket.

1 Trace pattern (page 62) onto paper. Apply square of fusible interfacing to wrong side of outer fabric square, following manufacturer's instructions. Pin pattern to interfaced fabric square. Cut on outer marked lines of pattern. Repeat for lining fabric.

2 Fold outer fabric piece in half, right sides together; pin. Stitch from the upper edge to point, ¼" (6 mm) from the raw edges. Repeat for the lining and heavyweight nonfusible interfacing, using ⅜" (1 cm) seam allowances.

3

4

3 Trim seam allowances close to stitching; trim point. Carefully press seam allowances to one side, using tip of iron.

4 Turn outer fabric piece right side out. Insert heavy-weight interfacing inside outer fabric basket; align seam allowances. Baste ⅛" (3 mm) from upper edge of basket.

5 Insert lining into basket, wrong sides together; align seam allowances. Carefully push lining deep into basket, using pointed object, such as a knitting needle. Pin lining to basket along upper edge. Trim any excess lining fabric even with upper edge of the basket. Stitch lining to basket at upper edge, using a short narrow zigzag stitch.

6 Apply liquid fray preventer to ends of ribbon or trim for basket hanger. Pin trim to each side of basket at upper edge; hand-stitch in place. Hand-stitch trim over seamline on outside of basket, if desired. Handstitch or machine-stitch trim to outside and inside of basket at upper edge to conceal raw edges; apply liquid fray preventer to cut ends of trim.

7 Stitch button, tassel, or beads to the lower edge of the basket, if desired, using thread that matches the embellishment. Fill the basket with miniature ornaments, packages, or candies.

1 **Pieced basket.** Fuse knit interfacing to the backs of four or five fabric scraps for pieced outer basket, following manufacturer's instructions. Cut a straight line on one side of each of two fabric scraps. Pin the fabrics right sides together, aligning straight edges. Stitch ¼" (6 mm) from raw edges. Press the seam allowances to one side.

2 Cut straight line at an angle along one side of pieced strip, and cut a straight line on a third scrap of fabric. Pin fabrics right sides together, aligning straight edges. Stitch ¼" (6 mm) from raw edges. Press seam allowances to one side. Repeat to stitch together a total of four or five fabrics as desired. Follow steps 1 to 7, opposite and above, using pieced fabric for outer fabric; omit reference to interfacing outer fabric square in step 1.

6

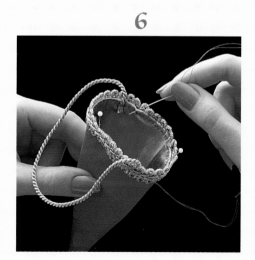

1

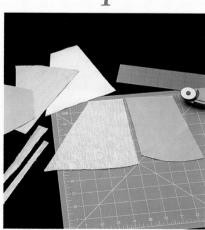

2

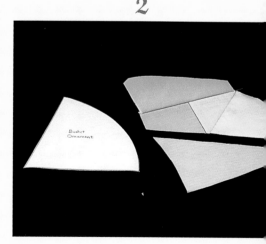

Love Hearts

Another popular Scandinavian decoration which began in Denmark and spread to Sweden is the Love Heart. This woven, heart-shaped basket, often filled with sweets, is hung on the Christmas tree, in windows of homes and shops, and as festoons above the streets. Danish hearts are traditionally interwoven of red and white paper. While these are the colors of the Danish flag, symbolic meanings have also been attached to the colors: red for love and white for purity. Swedish hearts are more diverse in color, often weaving red with green.

How to make a Love Heart Ornament

Love heart ornaments also can be made from fabric. For the outside of the heart basket, use two coordinating Christmas prints or two solid-color fabrics. Select a fabric in a coordinating color to line the inside of the heart basket. For variety, make several heart ornaments in different fabrics, both solid and printed. Use braid trim or ribbon for the hangers.

Materials

- ⅛ yd. (0.15 m) each of two coordinating fabrics, in cotton or cotton blends.
- ⅛ yd. (0.15 m) fabric, in cotton or cotton blend, for lining.
- ⅝ yd. (0.6 m) narrow braid trim or ribbon, for hanger and bow.
- Paper-backed fusible web.
- Thick white craft glue.

1 Trace partial template for heart basket ornament (page 62) onto paper, with dotted line of template on fold of paper. Cut on solid line to make full-size template.

2 Draw two 2½" × 7½" (6.5 × 19.3 cm) rectangles on paper side of paper-backed fusible web. Apply fusible web to lining, following the manufacturer's directions. Cut out rectangles.

2

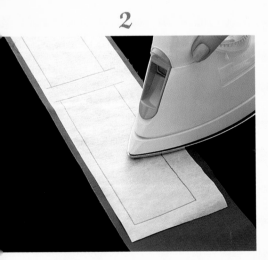

3

4

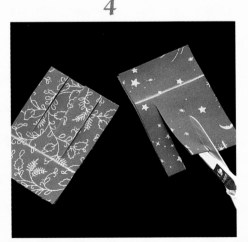

3 Remove paper backing, and fuse lining pieces to contrasting outer fabrics. Trim outer fabric to match lining pieces.

4 Fold each rectangle in half crosswise; press. Mark points along fold at ⅝" (1.5 cm) intervals, using chalk. Mark chalk line parallel to, and 2½" (6.5 cm) from, the fold. Clip fabric from the marked points at fold to marked chalk line.

5 Weave red and green strips together by alternately inserting loops through each other.

6 Continue weaving red and green strips together as shown.

7 Place heart template over basket, aligning point of basket with point of heart; pin. Trim away the excess fabric around curve of heart.

8 Secure a 9" (23 cm) length of ribbon for handle on each side of heart basket between fabric strips, using glue. Tie two bows from the remaining ribbon; glue bows to each side of basket.

5

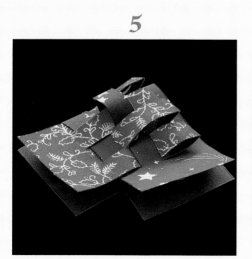

6

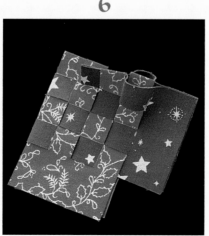

7

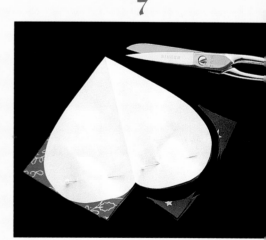

Victorian

When Prince Albert of Germany married Queen Victoria of England in 1840, he brought with him to Windsor Castle many of the Christmas traditions of his native country. He brought the first Christmas tree into their home in 1841 and decorated it with candles, fruits, gingerbread, and other sweets. Other wealthy families adopted the tradition, and because they lived in such opulent times, decorated their trees very extravagantly. Ornaments included such items as dolls, miniature musical instruments, costume jewelry, and expensive laces. The royal family celebrated Christmas with elaborate decorations and feasts with an emphasis on family and children, kindness toward others, and charity. Anything the royal family did was copied by the people of England, so the customs soon became quite fashionable, and eventually made their way to America.

How to make a Charm Ornament

Visit the romance of the Victorian era with these two ornaments. Cover Styrofoam® forms with delicate netting or narrow ribbon. Adorn them with metal or resin Victorian charms, beads, and decorative trims, such as cording, ribbon, and gimp. Secure embellishments with craft glue or with escutcheon or dressmaker pins, for quick and easy finishing.

Materials

- Styrofoam form, 3½" to 4" (9 to 10 cm) tall.
- Acrylic paint, in desired colors.
- ¾ yd. (0.7 m) cording, lace, or ribbon.
- ½ yd. (0.5 m) tulle or sparkle illusion.
- Victorian charms as desired; hot glue gun.
- Beads and sequins as desired; straight or escutcheon pins.

1 Paint form as desired; allow to dry. Tie small knots at trim ends to prevent raveling, if necessary. Tie square knot to form 3" (7.5 cm) loop at trim center. Set form on 15" (38 cm) tulle square. Gather tulle firmly at top. Place trim knot at back; tie bow in front to secure tulle.

2 Paint resin charms, if desired. Apply charms to front and back as desired, using hot glue. Apply beads as desired, using brass pins.

1

2

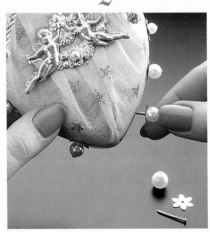

How to make a Ribbon Ball Ornament

Materials

- 10 yd. (9.15 m) ribbon, ¼" to ⅜" (6 mm to 1 cm) wide.
- 3" (7.5 cm) Styrofoam ball.
- Craft glue.
- Two or more beads as desired.
- Straight or escutcheon pins as desired.
- Embellishments as desired.

1 Secure end of ribbon to ball, using glue. Wrap ribbon around ball, overlapping ribbon slightly, until ball is covered. Pull end of ribbon tight; secure at top of ball, using glue. Hold firmly until dry.

2 Leave 6" (15 cm) ribbon tail, for loop; glue end to top, forming loop. Pin bead, using straight or escutcheon pin, at top and bottom to prevent ribbon layers from slipping. Secure additional trims or beads as desired.

1

2

How to make a Potpourri Ball Ornament

Victorian ornaments, such as potpourri balls and paper fans, bring a touch of nostalgia to the tree. The potpourri balls, made from bridal illusion, and the elegant paper fans, made from paper lace or wrapping paper, are trimmed with embellishments for romantic appeal.

1 Place potpourri in center of 12" (30.5 cm) circle of bridal illusion. Gather illusion around potpourri to form ball; secure by twisting wire around gathers.

2 Push one end of wire into center of gathered illusion; fold over and twist to form loop. Trim excess wire.

3 Insert ribbon through wire loop; tie ends together. Glue lace around potpourri ball, overlapping ends. Add embellishments as desired.

Materials

- Potpourri, 1 cup (250 mL) for each ornament.
- Bridal illusion, or tulle.
- 3" (7.5 cm) length of 24-gauge brass wire.
- 9" (23 cm) length of narrow ribbon, for hanging ornament.
- 5" (12.5 cm) length of pregathered lace, about 1" (2.5 cm) wide.
- Embellishments as desired, such as dried rosebuds, statice, pearl strands, and ribbon.

2

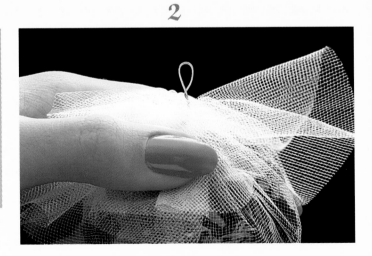

How to make a Paper Fan Ornament

Materials

- 12" (30.5 cm) length of paper lace, 2½" to 4" (6.5 to 10 cm) wide; or 12" (30.5 cm) length of wrapping paper, 4" (10 cm) wide.
- Metallic or pearlescent acrylic paint, optional.
- 9" (23 cm) length of narrow ribbon or cord, for hanging ornament.
- Embellishments as desired, such as dried rosebuds, statice, pearl strands, and ribbon.

1 Apply a light coat of metallic or pearlescent paint to right side of paper, if desired; thin paint as necessary, for a transparent effect. Fold paper in ½" to ⅝" (1.3 to 1.5 cm) accordion pleats, making first fold to back side of paper. Trim excess paper at end, if necessary.

2 Glue pleats together at lower edge; clamp glued ends together with clothespin until dry. Open pleats into fan.

3 Lace ribbon through a hole in top of fan; knot ends together to form hanger. Glue embellishments at lower end of fan.

1

2

39

Christmas Spider

One Christmas Eve long ago, a mother busily cleaned her house in preparation for the the coming of the Christ Child and the next day's celebration. As was the custom, after her children had gone to bed, she carefully decorated the Christmas tree, anticipating the delight on her children's faces when they would see it for the first time the next morning. When all the ornaments were in place, she took one last adoring look, closed the doors to the room, and went to bed.

In the dark of the night, the friendly spiders, who had been chased from their webs by the mother's thorough cleaning, crept back into the room to steal a peek at the lovely tree. Captivated by the beauty of the ornaments, the spiders crept from one branch to another admiring each pretty bauble, all the while spinning their webs until the entire tree was shrouded with the gossamer threads.

When the Christ Child arrived early the next morning, he was pleased that God's lowly creatures had enjoyed the tree so much, but he knew the mother would be greatly dismayed after working so hard to decorate it. One touch of his hand turned the webs to shimmering silver and gold, making the tree even more beautiful than before. Ever after, it has been a custom to drape the Christmas tree with silver and gold tinsel and to hang a spider ornament somewhere in its branches.

How to make a Christmas Spider Ornament

Representing the small creatures of the animal kingdom, this sparkling spider takes its place amid the evergreen branches. Its head and body are wooden beads covered with the large size of Tiny Glass Marbles, sold in craft stores and available in several colors. Its bendable legs are simply bugle beads strung on wires. Such an elegant ornament, surely you'll want to hang it in plain sight where it can be admired, prompting you to retell the legend of the Christmas spider.

Materials

- Peel n Stick™ double-sided adhesive tape.
- 12 mm wood bead for head.
- 16 mm wood bead for body.
- Mat knife.
- Tiny Glass Marbles by Halcraft USA, large size.
- 2" (5 cm) gold jewelry head pin.
- Two small gold beads, slightly larger than holes in wood beads.
- Round-nose jewelry pliers.
- Gold jewelry wire, 24- or 26-gauge.
- Small crystal bugle beads.
- Metallic thread for hanger.

1

2

1 Wrap double-sided adhesive strip around large wood bead; remove paper backing. Repeat around bead until entire surface is covered. Repeat for small wood bead. Cross-cut ends with mat knife; press adhesive into holes.

2 Roll beads in Tiny Marbles until completely covered. Roll gently in hands to smooth and secure. Fill in any bare spots.

3 Insert head pin through small gold bead, small wood bead, large wood bead, and second small gold bead. Bend loop in end of head pin, using round-nose pliers; allow small space between wood beads for adding legs.

4 Cut four pieces of wire, 4" (10 cm) long. Form tiny loop at one end of each, using pliers. Insert each wire through 14 bugle beads. Form tiny loops in wires ½" (1.3 cm) from last bead; trim off excess wire.

5 Separate bugle beads, so space is in center. Wrap four wires together around space between head and body, forming legs. Curve and separate legs on underside of spider.

6 Wrap 10" (25.5 cm) length of metallic thread around spider middle; knot ends together, forming loop for hanging.

3

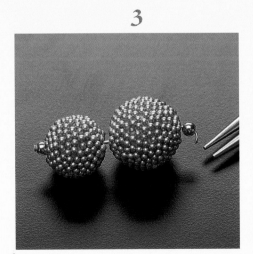

4

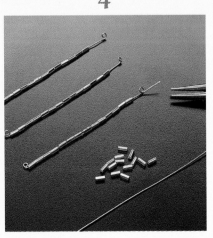

5

43

Bells

Bells and noisemakers of all kinds were first used by pagans when festivals for the winter solstice included making as much noise as possible to frighten away evil spirits in the darkness of winter. Later believed to have holy powers, bells were rung during storms to protect against lightning and tolled during funeral processions to ward off evil. Over time, bells became associated with celebrations. Bells toll all over the world on Christmas Eve, ringing out the good news of the arrival of Christ.

How to make a Jingle Bell Ornament

Jingle bells have long been associated with Christmas. Whether hung on leather straps from a horse-drawn sleigh or simply dangled from the front door knob, their merry tinkling chimes announce holiday visitors. Gold jingle bell clusters that resemble small bunches of grapes are a symbol of hospitality and joy. Quick and easy to make, they are perfect for hanging on the Christmas tree, adorning Christmas packages, or accenting a wreath.

Materials

- 8" (20.5 cm) length of 24-gauge brass wire.
- Nine ⅝" (1.5 cm) jingle bells.
- 10" (25.5 cm) length of ribbon, ⅝" (1.5 cm) wide.
- Needlenose pliers.
- 9" (23 cm) length of gold cord, for hanging ornament.
- 8" (20.5 cm) length of ribbon, ¼" (6 mm) wide.
- Craft glue.

46

1 Insert about 1" (2.5 cm) of wire through hanger of bell; twist to secure.

2 Insert other end of wire into remaining bells. First bell will be at bottom of ornament.

3 Make bow by folding ⅝" (1.5 cm) ribbon back and forth, forming a loop on each side; secure above top bell by wrapping wire around center of bow several times.

4 Form wire loop above bow with pliers, twisting wire to secure; trim excess wire.

5 Insert gold cord through the wire loop; tie ends. Tie ¼" (6 mm) ribbon in small bow; glue at center of looped bow, concealing the wire.

2

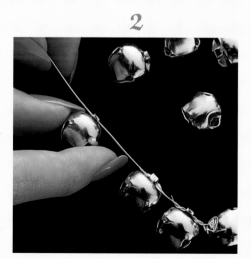

4

5

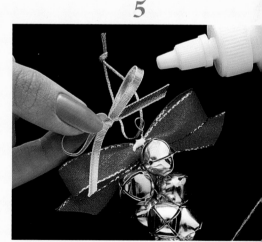

Moravian Stars

Prominently figured in the Christmas story, the Star of Bethlehem which guided the Wise Men to the manger needs little explanation about its importance and meaning. In remembrance of the story and as a symbol of high hopes and high ideals, a star is often placed at the top of a Christmas tree.

Stars of various shapes have been used over the centuries in Christmas customs and celebrations. One elaborate many-pointed star, known as the Moravian star, originated in Germany over 150 years ago. Pieter Verbeek remembered making it as a young Moravian boy during evening handicraft sessions. He began producing the star commercially from his home. His son, Harry, later founded the Herrnhut star factory and grew it into a thriving business, exporting Moravian stars to all parts of the world. Today the star is also known as the Advent star, as it became a custom in Germany and other countries to hang the star in the church on the first Sunday in Advent.

How to make a Moravian Star

Using simple folding techniques, turn strips of paper or ribbon into delicate, dimensional Moravian star ornaments. Each star ornament is made from four strips of paper or ribbon. The width of the paper strips or ribbon determines the size of the ornament. Use the chart at right to help determine the width and length of the strips needed to make a star of the desired size.

For paper stars, select papers of medium weight, such as parchment papers and gift-wrapping papers. To make gift-wrapping paper decorative on both sides, fuse two sheets together, using lightweight paper-backed fusible web. Test to be sure the paper does not become too stiff to crease easily.

For ribbon stars, select ribbons that are attractive on both sides and that hold a crease well, such as some craft and metallic ribbons; avoid satin or taffeta ribbons.

Size Chart

Approximate Size	Width of Strip	Length of Strip	Yardage Required
2" (5 cm)	1/2" (1.3 cm)	15" (38 cm)	1¾ yd. (1.6 m)
3" to 3½" (7.5 to 9 cm)	⅝" to ¾" (1.5 to 2 cm)	18" (46 cm)	2 yd. (1.85 m)
4½" (11.5 cm)	1" (2.5 cm)	27" (68.5 cm)	3 yd. (2.75 m)
6½" to 7" (16.3 to 18 cm)	1⅜" to 1½" (3.5 to 3.8 cm)	36" (91.5 cm)	4 yd. (3.7 m)
9" (23 cm)	2" (5 cm)	46" (117 cm)	5⅛ yd. (4.7 m)

1

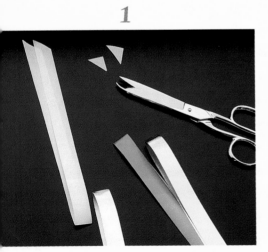

2

3

Materials

- Paper or ribbon, amount depending on size of star desired (see chart, opposite).
- Lightweight paper-backed fusible web, for use with papers that are decorative on one side only.
- Thick craft glue; decorative thread or cording, for hanger.

1 Fold each of the four strips in half; trim ends to points. Place two folded strips vertically with the tips of the left strip pointing up and tips of right strip pointing down.

2 Place the left vertical strip between layers of a third strip, positioning it near fold of third strip. Place ends of third strip between the layers of the right vertical strip.

3 Weave the fourth strip below third strip by placing ends of right vertical strip between layers of fourth strip. Place ends of fourth strip between layers of left vertical strip. Pull ends tightly.

4 Fold top layer of left vertical strip down; crease. Rotate woven square one-quarter turn clockwise.

5 Repeat step 4 to fold the next two top layers down; insert fourth strip between layers of the lower left square as shown. Crease and rotate one-quarter turn clockwise.

6 Fold upper right strip over itself at 45° angle as shown; crease. *(continued)*

4

5

6

7 Fold same strip over itself at 45° angle as shown; crease.

8 Fold same strip to left, aligning folded edges; insert end of strip between layers of upper right square to make one star point. Rotate woven square one-quarter turn clockwise.

9 Repeat steps 6 to 8 to make four star points.

10 Turn star over. Repeat steps 6 to 8 to make four more star points, for a total of eight star points.

11 Lift horizontal strip at upper right corner to the left, out of the way. Fold up vertical strip at lower right; crease.

12 Fold same strip over itself at 45° angle as shown; crease. Grasp end of strip; keep this side of the strip facing up as you complete step 13.

13 Turn the strip counterclockwise; insert end of strip between layers of upper left square. Strip will come out through star point; open point of star with finger or tip of scissors, if necessary. Pull tight to make star point that projects upward.

7   8   11   12

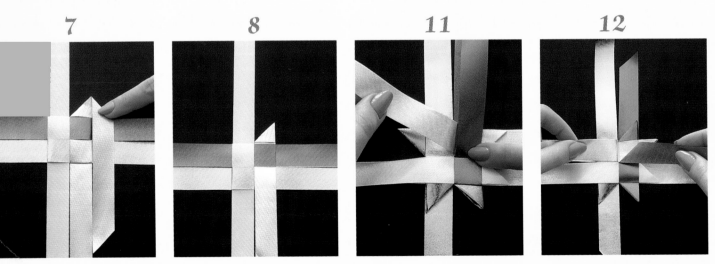

14 Rotate star one-quarter turn clockwise and repeat steps 11 to 13 to make four projecting star points.

15 Turn star over. Repeat steps 11 to 14 to make four additional projecting star points. Trim ends of strips even with edge of outer star points. Secure by applying dot of glue to both sides of ends, if necessary.

16 Thread needle; insert needle through star between two outer points. Knot ends of thread for hanger.

13

14

15

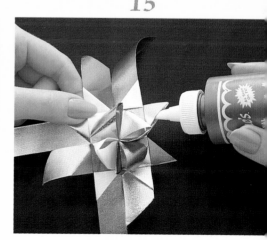

Molded Beeswax

Christmas cookie bakers in 16th-century Germany invented the idea of molding beeswax into ornaments. The *lebkuchen* they baked was made of gingerbread and pressed into intricate wooden molds that depicted religious scenes and had much symbolic meaning. The recipe called for honey, which they removed from honeycombs gathered from the wild. Perhaps while waiting for the cookies to bake, people passing time by manipulating the leftover beeswax in their hands pressed it into the cookie molds and were pleased with the impression it left. They began molding the beeswax pieces as decorations for their homes for Christmas. Not only did they enjoy the detail and symbolism of the pretty designs, but the ornaments also filled their rooms with the soft honey scent of the beeswax. In the late 17th century, German immigrants to America brought this art form to eastern Pennsylvania. As the craft evolved, the ornaments were often painted or gilded. The ornaments became treasured family heirlooms passed from generation to generation. There are antique beeswax ornaments in some German museums today that are over 300 years old.

How to make Molded Beeswax Ornaments

Molded beeswax ornaments, a nostalgic memento of the Christmas season, are versatile as candle accents, napkin ring favors for dinner party guests, or a unique garland for a tabletop display. Beeswax is simply melted in boiling bags and poured into intricately detailed flexible polymer molds. The molds are available separately or in multiple sets, enabling you to pour several ornaments at a time. When cooled, the ornaments can be trimmed with ribbons, berries, sprigs of greenery, or dried flowers. They also can be painted with acrylic paints or accented with pearlized powders or wax-based metallics.

Materials

- Freezer paper.
- Flexible polymer ornament molds.
- 9" (23 cm) length of ribbon or cord, for each hanger, if making individual ornaments.
- Beeswax pellets.
- Boiling bag; clothespin.
- Large saucepan; water.

- Acrylic paints, wax-based metallics, or pearlized powders; small paintbrush.
- 1 yd. (0.95 m) narrow decorative cord in desired length, for garland.
- Embellishments, such as narrow ribbons, berries, sprigs of greenery, or dried flowers.

1

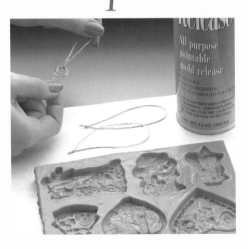

1 Cover work surface with freezer paper, shiny side up. Place molds on freezer paper. Knot ends of ribbon or cord together, for hangers.

2 Pour beeswax pellets into melting bag. Roll top down, and secure with clothespin. Submerge in pan of boiling water.

3 Remove boiling bag from water when wax has melted; towel off any dripping water. Remove clothespin; slowly pour beeswax into candle mold, filling to top. Insert knotted end of hanger into

beeswax at top of each mold, working quickly before wax hardens. Allow to cool.

4 Remove cooled ornaments from molds. Paint or apply pearlized powders as desired.

5 **Garland.** Tie knots at each end of 1 yd. (0.95 m) of narrow decorative cord; tie four knots evenly spaced between ends. Pour melted wax into molds. Quickly insert one knot into beeswax at top of each mold; allow to cool. Remove garland from molds; embellish as desired.

3

4

5

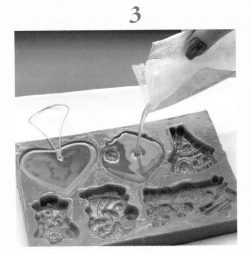

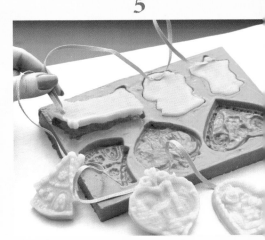

Christmas Crackers

While on a trip to Paris in 1840, Tom Smith, a wedding cake baker from London, discovered the new French treat called "bonbons." After returning to London, he began selling these sugarcoated almonds wrapped in a twist of paper. When he noticed that the candy was a favorite gift between young sweethearts, Smith began hiding love mottos inside the wrappings, modeling the idea after Chinese fortune cookies. Then one day in 1846, while standing by his crackling fireplace, Smith was inspired to develop a way to add even more excitement to his candy. He devised a strip of paper coated with a very mild explosive that would spark and crack as the candy wrapper was pulled apart. Tom Smith's cracking sweets soon became the most popular candy. Eventually the outer wrapper became more decorative, and small gifts were hidden inside, making them a suitable Christmas treat. By 1900 Tom Smith had sold more than thirteen million of his famous crackers. The Christmas cracker became an essential part of the holiday in England and a lasting custom that is enjoyed by children and adults alike.

How to make a Christmas Cracker

Fashioned after Tom Smith's original Christmas cracker, this version is quick and easy to make, and can be hung on the tree or used as a table favor at holiday gatherings. It can be personalized with the addition of a nameplate or decorated with Christmas stickers, ribbons, or tiny bells. The cracker snapper is a miniature firecracker in the center of a string that "explodes" when the string is pulled. Look for these snappers in magic stores and fun shops. To open the cracker, grab the ends tightly and pull with a quick jerk. Even without the snapper, there will be a mild popping sound as the cracker opens to reveal its hidden prize.

Materials

- Cardboard tubes from wrapping paper.
- Craft knife; scissors.
- Lighweight gift-wrapping paper or crepe paper.
- Decorative-blade scissors, optional.
- Double-stick tape.
- Cracker snapper; hot glue gun, optional.
- Gift-wrap ribbon.
- Small gifts or treats for filling cracker.
- Decorative trims, such as stickers or seals.
- Metallic string for hanger.

1 Cut two 4" (10 cm) sections of cardboard tube, using a craft knife; cut one piece in half. Cut a piece of paper 6" × 11" (15 × 28 cm); trim short ends, using decorative-blade scissors, if desired.

2 Place paper face down on work surface. Align tubes to long edge of paper, centering large tube and aligning small tubes to short ends of paper. Secure center tube to paper, using double-stick tape.

3 Tie small knots in snapper ends; place snapper alongside tubes. Secure knots to paper with dots of hot glue; allow to cool. Roll paper around tubes and secure, using double-stick tape; leave spaces between tubes untaped.

4 Pinch paper together in gap between tubes at one end; tie tightly with ribbon.

5 Fill center tube with treats and gifts. Repeat step 4 for opposite end. Apply decorative trims to center of cracker as desired. Remove short tubes from ends and use for making additional crackers.

6 Tie metallic string over ribbon at one end for hanging on tree.

2

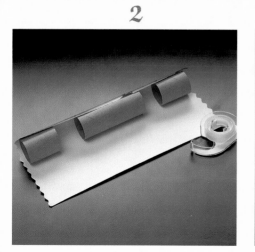

3

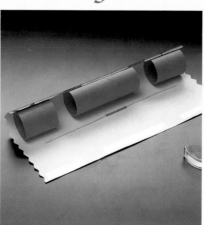

5

61

*P*atterns

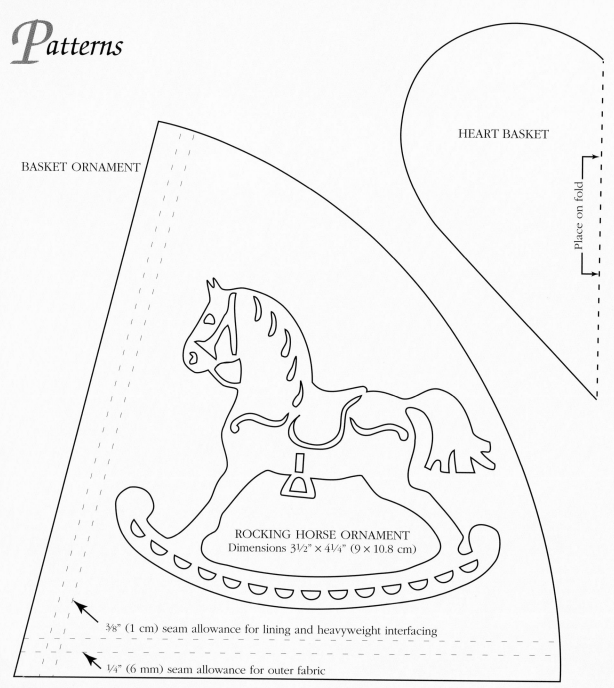

BASKET ORNAMENT

HEART BASKET

Place on fold

ROCKING HORSE ORNAMENT
Dimensions 3½" × 4¼" (9 × 10.8 cm)

⅜" (1 cm) seam allowance for lining and heavyweight interfacing

¼" (6 mm) seam allowance for outer fabric

PACKAGE ORNAMENT
Dimensions
4⅝" × 3½"
(11.7 × 9 cm)

Place on fold

Place on fold

DOVE GARLAND

Place on fold

Place on fold

PARTRIDGE ORNAMENT

Place on fold

CANDLE ORNAMENT
Dimensions
4¼" × 3¼" (10.8 × 8.2 cm)

Dimensions
6⅛" × 6¾"
(15.4 × 17 cm)